I Need You, Dear Dragon

Margaret Hillert

Illustrated by David Helton

MODERN CURRICULUM PRESS

© **1985 MODERN CURRICULUM PRESS, INC.**
13900 Prospect Road, Cleveland, Ohio 44136.

Softcover edition published simultaneously in Canada by
Globe/Modern Curriculum Press, Toronto.

Library of Congress Cataloging in Publication Data

Hillert, Margaret.
    I need you, dear dragon.

    Summary: Dear dragon feels somewhat rejected when his
master's new baby sister comes home from the hospital,
but love and reassurance put things right.
    (1. Babies — Fiction.   2. Dragons — Fiction)
I. Helton, David, ill.   II. Title.
PZ7.H558Iam   1984   (E)   83-22069

ISBN 0-8136-5634-6   **Paperback**
ISBN 0-8136-5134-4   **Hardbound**

20 19 18 17 16 15   06 05 04 03 02 01 00

Here comes the car.
Oh, here comes the car.
I see Mother.
Mother is home.

Mother, Mother.
Now you are home.
That is good.

6

Is that the baby?
I want to see it.
Oh, I want to see it!

Oh, my. Oh, my.
A little, little baby.

What a pretty baby!
What a pretty baby it is.
Look, look.

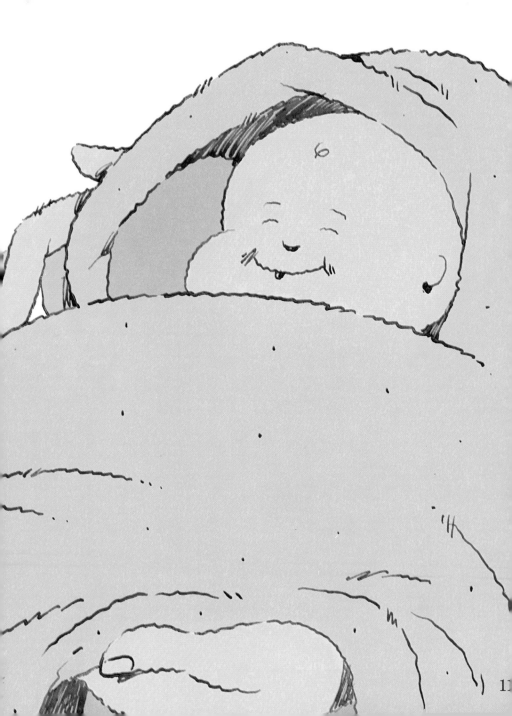

In here.
In here.
This is where we go.

This is something for
the baby —

and this —

and this.

Father, Father.
Can I have the baby?
I want the baby.

My, what a pretty one.
So little, little.
I like you, little baby.

Here, Mother.
This is a good little baby.
I like her.

Oh, there you are.
You did not come in.
We want you to come in.

See.
Here is something that
looks like you.
It is for the baby.

The baby will like it.
Yes, yes.
The baby will like it.

Come here. Come here.
You can do something here.
Come on.
Oh, come on.

See now.
Look what you can do.
This is a good thing for
you to do.

Look at that.
The baby likes you.
And I like you, too.
I do. I do.

The baby is little.
Too little to play with me now.
But you and I can play.

We can play and have fun.
Come on with me.
Come on and play.
Run, run, run.

Here you are with me.
And here I am with you.
I need you.
I need you, dear dragon.

Margaret Hillert, author and poet, has written many books for young readers. She is a former first-grade teacher and lives in Birmingham, Michigan.

I Need You, Dear Dragon uses the 60 words listed below.

a	good	now	want
am			we
and	have	oh	what
are	her	on	where
at	here	one	will
	home		with
baby		play	
but	I	pretty	yes
	in		you
can	is	run	
car	it		
come		see	
	like	so	
dear	little	something	
did	look		
do		that	
dragon	me	the	
	Mother	there	
Father	my	thing	
for		this	
fun	need	to	
	not	too	
go			